SPURS
100

TRANSWORLD PUBLISHERS
61–63 Uxbridge Road, London W5 5SA
A Random House Group Company
www.transworldbooks.co.uk

First published in Great Britain
in 2014 by Bantam Press
an imprint of Transworld Publishers

Created and compiled by Will Brooks and Tim Glynne-Jones with Martin Cloake
(Spurs) copyright © Will Brooks and Tim Glynne-Jones 2014

Design by David Ashford

Visit www.100nil.com for more indefensible screamers.

A CIP catalogue record for this book
is available from the British Library.

ISBN 9780593074572

Addresses for Random House Group Ltd companies outside the UK can be found
at: www.randomhouse.co.uk
The Random House Group Ltd Reg. No. 954009

The Random House Group Limited supports the Forest Stewardship Council®
(FSC®), the leading international forest-certification organisation. Our
books carrying the FSC label are printed on FSC®-certified paper. FSC is the
only forest-certification scheme supported by the leading environmental
organisations, including Greenpeace. Our paper procurement policy can be
found at www.randomhouse.co.uk/environment

Typeset in Flama

Printed and bound in Germany

2 4 6 8 10 9 7 5 3 1

SPURS
100
ARSENAL
0

Created and compiled by
Will Brooks and Tim Glynne-Jones

with Martin Cloake

BANTAM PRESS

LONDON · TORONTO · SYDNEY · AUCKLAND · JOHANNESBURG

The Glory Name

Spurs took their name from heroic Harry Hotspur, the nickname of the swashbuckling Henry Percy, 11th Duke of Northumberland, who was immortalized in Shakespeare's *Henry IV*.

Arsenal took their name from a factory.

Originally starting life as 'Dial Square', the name changed to 'Royal Arsenal', then to 'Woolwich Arsenal' after the munitions factory, and finally to 'Arsenal' when they moved the franchise from south to north London. Calling them the Woolwich Nomads still winds 'em up.

~~Dial Square~~

~~Royal Arsenal~~

~~Woolwich~~ Arsenal

1-0

Null and Void

Even from the beginning it's been 'same old Arsenal, always cheating'. Arsenal are the only club in English football's top division who did not reach their position on merit. When football restarted after the First World War in 1919, Arsenal were voted in after some behind-the-scenes shenanigans, taking the place of Spurs. So technically nothing they have won since 1919 really counts.

2-0

Bereft of Life

On the day Arsenal inveigled Spurs out of their
rightful place in the top division in 1919, the
parrot that had lived at White Hart Lane since
being brought back from a South American tour
by the players fell off its perch and died.
It's rumoured this is where the phrase 'sick as a
parrot' comes from, and has earned Arsenal the
unofficial nickname of 'parrot killers'.

3-0

Same Old Arsenal . . .

Saturday 19 November 1887, Tottenham Marshes, friendly

Spurs **2**

(goalscorers unrecorded)

Royal Arsenal **1**

(match abandoned after 75 minutes)

The first match between Spurs and Arsenal was played in 1887. Spurs are coasting to victory at 2-1 with 15 minutes to go when Arsenal – or whatever they were called at the time – moan to the ref about bad light and get the game called off. It's the first recorded instance of the excuse: 'I did not see the incident.'

4–0

The Double

1961
1971

In 1961, Spurs became the first team to win the modern League and Cup double, with a thrilling brand of football that saw them dubbed 'the team of the century'. When Arsenal caught up 10 years later, their style of play was deadly dull. Boring, boring Arsenal.

5-0

That's Entertainment

DIVISION 1 1960/61

		P	W	D	L	F	A	Pts
1	Tottenham Hotspur	42	31	4	7	115	55	66
2	Sheffield Wednesday	42	23	12	7	78	47	58
3	Wolverhampton Wanderers	42	25	7	10	103	75	57
4	Burnley	42	22	7	13	102	77	51
5	Everton	42	22	6	14	87	69	50
6	Leicester City	42	18	9	15	87	70	45
7	Manchester United	42	18	9	15	88	76	45
8	Blackburn Rovers	42	15	13	14	77	76	43
9	Aston Villa	42	17	9	16	78	77	43
10	West Bromwich Albion	42	18	5	19	67	71	41
11	Arsenal	42	15	11	16	77	85	41

When Spurs won the Double they finished with most
points, most goals, most wins and most away wins
in top-flight history. They also enjoyed the most
consecutive wins from the start of the season
(a top-flight record that still stands).
When Arsenal sneaked the Double 10 years later,
they didn't even score the most goals in the division.

6—0

FFS!

Tuesday 24 April 1900, Manor Ground Plumstead,
Southern and District Combination

Woolwich Arsenal **2**

v

Spurs **1**

(goalscorers unrecorded)

It's the second derby played in a week, with Spurs
having won the previous game 4-2.
On 75 minutes, with Arsenal leading 2-1, the
game is called off. This time, the excuse isn't
'bad light' but 'bad language'. The result stands.
While records don't show who the potty-
mouthed players were, the ruse of ending a
match early when it suits them has already been
established by the cheating Gooners.

```
7-0
```

DNA

> 'The game is about glory, about doing things in style, with a flourish, about going out and beating the other lot, not waiting for them to die of boredom.'

DANNY BLANCHFLOWER (SPURS)

> 'A team can attack for too long.'
> **HERBERT CHAPMAN (ARSENAL)**

Record Attendance

75,038

73,707

9–0

Lowest Average Attendance

13,370

4,460

10–0

League of Their Own

In 1901, Spurs became the first, and remain the only, non-league team to win the FA Cup when they beat Sheffield United in the final, just 19 years after the club's formation.

It took Arsenal 44 years to win the FA Cup – and even then it didn't count (see 2-0).

Euro Stars

In 1963 Spurs became the first British side to win a European trophy, beating Atlético Madrid 5-1 to lift the Cup Winners' Cup. Arsenal's first European trophy was the Inter-Cities Fairs Cup in 1970, a competition not recognized as a major trophy by UEFA.

European Trophies

3 ▯▯▯▾

1 ▾

Are Arsenal a true European team?
Persistent participation in the Champions League
with nothing to show for it – it's effectively a
place taken away from another more interesting
English team. Spurs, on the other hand, have won
three major European trophies: the Cup Winners'
Cup (1963) and the UEFA Cup twice (1972, 1984).
Arsenal have won just one major European pot,
the Cup Winners' Cup (1994).

13–0

Top Scorer

JIMMY GREAVES
266 goals

THIERRY HENRY
228 goals

14—0

First Win

Spurs **3**
Darnell, Minter, Humphreys

v

Woolwich Arsenal **1**
Chalmers

Spurs are known as the 'Flower of the South', non-League winners of the FA Cup and famed for their exciting, attacking play. Woolwich Arsenal still play on the site of an open sewer in south-east London, virtually bankrupt and soon to be relegated. Spurs triumph 3-1, gaining their first win against them in the League.

Mad Men

Spurs striker and all-round nice guy Gary Lineker has been endorsing Walkers crisps in a series of well made ads since 1995. Gormless Gooner striker Ian Wright, on the other hand, has been happy to put his face to a long list of unsavoury products, including Chicken Tonight.

16–0

Cup Final Songs

OSSIE'S DREAM
number 5

HOT STUFF
number 9

Spurs' 1981 FA Cup Final single *Ossie's Dream*
is widely considered a true classic, reaching
number 5 in the charts with its original lyrics
and a catchy melody that remains a popular
terrace chant today.
Arsenal have never charted higher than 9,
with the awful sub-karaoke reworking of
Donna Summer's *Hot Stuff* in 1998.

Top Of The Pops 2

NICE ONE CYRIL
number 14

GOOD OLD ARSENAL
number 16

The Cockerel Chorus's *Nice One Cyril* set the standard in the heyday of 70s football singles, reaching number 14 after it was released to celebrate Cyril Knowles and the boys reaching the League Cup Final in 1973.

It completely outclassed the droning *Good Old Arsenal*, which the Gunners had to have written for them by Jimmy Hill after they reached the FA Cup Final in 1971, and which only reached number 16 in the charts.

18–0

Footballing Karma

Spurs **2**
Bliss, Rutherford

v

Arsenal **1**
Cantrell

It takes Peter McWilliams' Spurs team just one season to reclaim their place in the top flight after Arsenal diddle them out of it, and in January comes the chance to wreak real revenge. This is the second great Spurs team, and they are intent on showing the authorities what a mistake they had made by giving their place in Division One to the interlopers from south London.
Spurs convincingly dispose of Arsenal and go on to finish above them in the table.

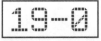

Banned!

In 1929, Arsenal chairman Henry Norris, the man who moved the club from south to north London and who was heavily involved in the club's dubious promotion to the top flight, was banned from football for life for financial dodgy dealing and flouting of FA rules.

No Spurs chairman has ever behaved quite so disgracefully. Not quite.

psssssssssssssssssssst!

Colours That Don't Run

Since adopting the famous lilywhite shirt and
blue shorts in 1898, Spurs have kept their home
kit consistently true to tradition. Arsenal's
shirt used to be all red, but white sleeves were
introduced by Herbert Chapman in 1933 because
the players were too stupid to recognize their
team mates without extra help.
And in a one-off marketing gimmick in 2005,
the shirts changed to a colour the club
embarrassingly insisted on calling 'redcurrant'.

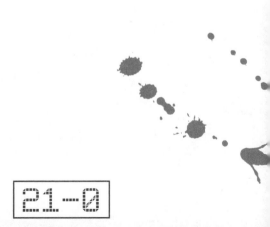

21—0

Your Shirt ... aaaargh!

Modern kit manufacturers have inflicted some horrors on football clubs, but Spurs have largely maintained their class. Arsenal, however, wore one of the vilest abominations in football history in 1991, with an away kit that came to be known as the 'tractor tyre' or 'bruised banana' – a nausea-inducing riot of yellow and blue zigzags.

22–0

'Oh what fun it is to see . . .'

Saturday 30 September 1922, Highbury, Division One

Arsenal **0**

v

Spurs **2**

Dimmock 2

With Spurs back in the top flight, it takes just
two attempts to beat the Gooners in their own
back yard. The great Jimmy Dimmock scores
both goals as the Lilywhites show that only one
team can legitimately call themselves north
London's finest.

23–0

Own Goal

Arsenal were once sponsored by Sega,
which is Italian for 'wank'.

Record Premier League Win

9-1
7-0

Jermain Defoe scored five goals in Spurs' record Premier League victory, a 9-1 thrashing of Wigan in 2009 that saw Spurs equal the highest number of goals to be scored in a single Premier League match. Arsenal's record Premier League win is the mere 7-0 defeat of Everton in 2005, repeated in 2006 against Middlesbrough.

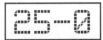

Spanner in the Works

Wednesday 31 January 1934, Highbury, Division One

Arsenal **1**
Bastin

v

Spurs **3**
Evans 2, Howe

The 1933/34 season will end with Arsenal securing the second of three successive dull League titles, but Spurs still put a spanner in the works, taking three of the four points on offer. In the first derby for six seasons in August 1933, newly promoted Spurs earned a draw at White Hart Lane and then, the following January, goals from Willie Evans and Les Howe not only secure local bragging rights but end the Gooners' unbeaten home record.

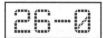

Latin Lesson

Audere est Facere

The Spurs motto *Audere est Facere* means 'To dare is to do' and epitomizes the club's swashbuckling spirit.

Arsenal's *Victoria Concordia Crescit*, or 'Victory comes from harmony', is not only bland psychobabble, it is also highly ironic considering the amount of unharmonious off- and on-the-pitch incidents the club has been involved in. Talking of which . . .

Victoria Concordia

27-0

'Good Old Arsenal . . .'

'. . . we're proud to say that name'

Really? Here's a snapshot of Arsenal's proud history:

Peter Storey: convictions for running *a brothel,* counterfeit coins and *importing* pornography

George Graham: found guilty by FA *of taking a £425,000 bung*

Ray Parlour: arrested after a punch-up *with a taxi driver in Hong Kong*

Paul Merson: needed rehab *after admitting cocaine and* alcohol addiction

Paul Davis: banned for breaking *Glenn Cockerill's jaw*

Andy Linighan: refusal to pay a taxi fare and *anti-semitic* abuse of the driver

Nicklas Bendtner: arrested for drink driving

David Hillier: stole luggage at an airport

Tony Adams: imprisoned for drink driving

Trainspotters

One of disgraced former Arsenal chairman
Henry Norris's dubious deals involved persuading
London Underground to rename Gillespie Road
underground station Arsenal station, presumably
because the gormless Gooners would never have
found their way to the ground otherwise.
Spurs fans have never had trouble finding their
way to the Lane.

29-0

Champion

Spurs **1**
Baily

v

Arsenal **0**

Arthur Rowe's Spurs team are the coming force in the English game, playing a style of push-and-run football that is sweeping the old guard before it. Old masters Newcastle are destroyed 7-0 in November and, just over a month later, Spurs tame table-topping Arsenal. It is 1-0 to the Tottenham on this occasion, thanks to a goal from inside-forward Eddie Baily – a narrow win but a giant step towards the League title.

Anagram-a-ding-dong

B O R E S

A L L

B U T

L O C A L

F A N

(Arsenal Football Club)

31-0

Fastest Premiership Goal

9 seconds

Ledley King v Bradford City, 9 December 2000

20 seconds

Theo Walcott v QPR, 4 May 2013

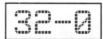

32–0

Bill's First

Saturday 16 January 1960, White Hart Lane, Division One

Spurs **3**
R Smith, Allen 2

v

Arsenal **0**

It's the first home derby for Spurs manager
Bill Nicholson, and a taste of what is to come.
Goals from Bobby Smith and Les Allen give Spurs
a convincing victory.
By the end of the season Arsenal are languishing
near the foot of the table, while third-placed
Spurs are increasingly convinced they can make
history the following season.

33–0

The Dark Side

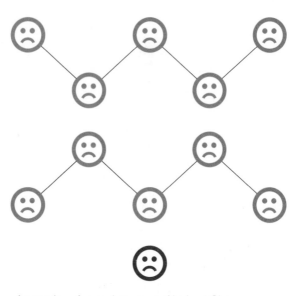

Legendary Arsenal manager Herbert Chapman was
an exciting player when he turned out for Spurs from
1905 to 1907, becoming leading goalscorer while
wearing a pair of flamboyant yellow boots.
After becoming Arsenal manager, he introduced the
dour and defensive WM formation, in which attacking
ambition was sacrificed by the introduction of an
extra defender to exploit the new offside rule.
The move was widely embraced by English football,
setting its development back a generation.

Singing for England

Paul Gascoigne, Gascoigne
He's done his country proud
We'll sing his name out loud
Paul Gascoigne, Gascoigne

If Lee Dixon can play for England
so can I

Glory Glory

One of the many classic Spurs chants is *Glory Glory Hallelujah*, made unique by Spurs fans for being the only ones not to insert the name of their team in the first line of the chorus.

Arsenal's most famous chant is *1-0 to the Arsenal*. Inspiring.

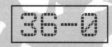

Name Shame

Winter slag

In one of the many defeats that have established Arsenal's laughable reputation in Europe, they lost to a team called Winterslag. The 1-0 defeat to the Belgian minnows came in the 1981/82 UEFA Cup competition. Spurs have never lost to a team with such an embarrassing name.

37–0

Highest Score

13-2

v Crewe Alexandra, 1960 (FA Cup)

12-0

v Ashford United, 1893 (FA Cup), and Loughborough Town, 1900 (Leagu

Arsenal claim a 26-1 win over a made-up Paris XI,
back in 1904: another example of trying to bend
the rules to boost their position, but they've never
scored even half that tally in a proper game.

38--0

Highbury High

Saturday 10 September 1960, Highbury, Division One

Arsenal **2**
Herd, Ward

v

Spurs **3**
Saul, Dyson, Allen

An away derby win is always welcome, but this one is extra special. It's win number seven in a run of 11 straight wins from the start of the season, establishing a top-flight record that still stands today.

Frank Saul on his debut and Terry Dyson put Spurs two up, then Spurs give Arsenal a chance to catch up, before Les Allen applies the coup de grace with a deft lob over Jack Kelsey.

A Highbury crowd of 59,868 gets the chance to admire the team of the century.

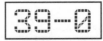

Double Double

Saturday 21 January 1961, White Hart Lane, Division One

Spurs **4**
Blanchflower, R Smith, Allen 2

Arsenal **2**
Haverty, Henderson

The win that completes the pair over the old enemy in the season in which Spurs complete the first Double in the modern game. Some 65,251 see Bill Nicholson's super Spurs give one of their best displays of an exceptional season. In the match report, the great John Arlott describes Spurs as a team 'wearing the air of conscious superiority that is now their accustomed strip'.

40-0

Marching In

Another of the finest sounds in football is the
massed ranks of the Spurs choir bellowing the
slow and measured version of
When the Spurs Go Marching In.
It certainly beats the unoriginal drone of
1-0 to the Arsenal.

MacNamara's Band

The classic Irish showband tune has long been adapted by lyrically gifted Spurs fans to go:

The whistle blows, the cockerel crows,
the Spurs are in the game
It's up to you, you Lilywhites, to play
the Tottenham way

Lyrically challenged Arsenal fans could only come up with:

1-0 to the Arsenal

Legends

Tottenham had Glenn Hoddle, who was 'Ghod'.
Arsenal had Tony Adams, who was 'Donkey'.

43–0

Dyson Cleans Up

Spurs **4**

Dyson 3, Allen

v

Arsenal **3**

Charles 2, Skirton

Double-winners Spurs have an early chance to
rub it in when Arsenal visit in the third game
of the 1961/62 season. A Terry Dyson hat-trick
confirms the Lilywhites' dominance.
Spurs will go on to retain the FA Cup, but miss
out on the League, finishing third – seven places
above Arsenal.

44–0

Bum Deal

Arse

Arsenal's name contains the word for a backside.

45–0

Pro Football

From Herbert Chapman's WM formation to George Graham's love of the long ball and offside trap, Arsenal's brand of negative anti-football helped send the English game into a tactical cul-de-sac.

Spurs managers John Cameron, Arthur Rowe and Bill Nicholson are widely credited with creating teams that not only thrilled the fans, but that changed the nature of English football, making it more able to compete with the technical superiority of overseas teams. There's winning, and there's winning with style and influence.

46–0

Party Like It's 1999

If you've got to lose, at least make sure
Arsenal lose out too. With nothing left to
play for at the end of the 1998/99 season,
Spurs arrived at Old Trafford knowing a win
or a draw would hand Arsenal the title.
Les Ferdinand snatched a shock lead before
David Beckham and Andy Cole made sure
the Reds secured the title, at the same time
ripping the trophy from the Gooners' grasp.

47-0

We Was Robbed!

Tuesday 15 October 1963, Highbury, Division One

Arsenal **4**

Eastham 2, Baker, Strong

v

Spurs **4**

Mackay, Smith 2, Greaves

A classic match in which the greatest Spurs side ever are denied a win by the kind of dubious refereeing decisions that help hang the 'Lucky Arsenal' tag around the Gooners' necks. With Spurs two up, a harsh penalty lets Arsenal back in the game, after which the ref disallows a Spurs goal that would have made it 4-1. In the end, a point is enough to take Spurs to the top of the table, but as the newspaper headlines say, 'Spurs were robbed'.

48-0

Another Bum Deal

Arse

Arsène Wenger's name also contains
the word for a backside.

49–0

Supercalifragilistic

Russian striker Roman Pavlyuchenko was honoured
with one of the best player chants ever.
It went:

*Supercalifragilistic
Roman Pavlyuchenko*

*Tottenham Hotspur's number 9
he's better than Shevchenko*

*When he has his breakfast he
puts vodka in his Kenko*

*Supercalifragilistic
Roman Pavlyuchenko*

It certainly knocks *1-0 to the Arsenal* into a cocked hat.

50–0

Goody Two Shoes

GARY LINEKER
never booked

ALAN SMITH
booked once

Both squeaky-clean goalscoring machines
for their clubs, but Lineker edges this battle
of the referees' pets.
These two were also strike partners at
Leicester City, where, of course, Lineker
outscored Smith.

51–0

Flower of the Spurs

Their style of play was more in keeping with the future than that of Arsenal.'

Spurs' Double-winning captain
Danny Blanchflower explains why,
when clubs were queuing up to sign him from
Aston Villa, he chose Spurs over Arsenal.

52-0

All Over Them

Spurs **3**

Greaves 2, Jones

v

Arsenal **1**

Sammels

Jimmy Greaves, the greatest goalscorer in the history of English football, bags two goals as Spurs complete the first of two victories over Arsenal in a season that ends with Bill Nicholson's side also lifting the FA Cup for the fifth time. Arsenal finish 10 points behind Spurs in the league.

53–0

Knowing When to Quit

Spurs' most successful manager, Bill Nicholson, created 'the team of the century', then gracefully retired at the top, a year after winning his last trophy, and was revered by Spurs fans ever after. Arsenal's most successful manager, Arsène Wenger, refused to call it a day, despite season after season of winning nothing, and left the Arsenal fans screaming for his head.

54-0

Nayim From the Halfway Line

Ronaldinho did it. Koeman managed it from 19 yards. But it's especially satisfying when a former Spurs player lobs Seaman.

The 1995 European Cup-Winners' Cup Final will live long in the memory of ex-Spurs midfielder Nayim, as well as Spurs fans everywhere. Stewart Houston had steered George Graham's anti-football side to the final after the former boss had been sacked for attempting to revive the club's history of dodgy dealing.

Arsenal ground the game towards a penalty shootout until, with just seconds to go, Nayim lobbed David Seaman to win the cup for Real Zaragoza. From how far out?

'Nayim from the halfway line.'

Spurs Against the Nazis

In the classic 1981 football yarn *Escape to Victory*, Tottenham Hotspur's midfield maestro Osvaldo Ardiles was cast as the Allied POW team's chief playmaker Carlos Rey. It was Rey's goal at the start of the second half that sparked the Allied team's fightback.

No Arsenal players were used in the making of this movie.

`56-0`

Cup Kings

Saturday 2 January 1982, White Hart Lane, FA Cup Round 3

Spurs **1**
Crooks

v

Arsenal **0**

The first post-war meeting between the two
teams in the FA Cup sees Spurs continue to
establish their early 1980s dominance.
Garth Crooks fires home the winner and Spurs
go on to lift the FA Cup for a record-breaking
seventh time.

We Love Martin Jol

In the final derby to be played at Highbury, Tottenham's Martin Jol and Arsenal's Arsène Wenger went eyeball to eyeball on the touchline after a fiery incident on the pitch. Afterwards, while Wenger whined about the game being stolen and the death of 'fair play', Jol defused the situation with typical good humour, endearing himself to Spurs fans while putting Wenger in his place.

'When Wenger squared up to me on the touchline,' said Jol, 'I had to hold myself back because he doesn't know how strong I am.'

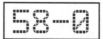

Why She Wore That Ribbon

She wore,
she wore,
She wore a yellow ribbon,
She wore a yellow ribbon,
In the merry month of May!
And when, I asked,
Oh why she wore that ribbon,
She said it's . . .
all thanks
to Spurs.

Ribbons are synonymous with Wembley cup
finals thanks to the wife of a Spurs director,
who tied blue and white ribbons on the FA Cup
after the club won the trophy in 1901.
So, unbeknownst to Arsenal fans, their
Wembley song is actually a nod to Spurs'
ownership of that little bit of football history.

Percentage of Major Cup Finals Won

75%
47%

When it comes to appearing in a major final*, Spurs are likely to win and Arsenal are likely to choke. The Lilywhites have lost just five finals out of 20, and were unbeaten in 11 between 1900 and 1973. Arsenal, on the other hand, have lost a whopping 16 out of 30. Which means that, although Spurs have reached fewer finals, they've won more.

* FA Cup , League Cup, Champions League, UEFA Cup and Cup Winners' Cup finals.

Back on Top

Monday 12 April 1982, Highbury, Division One

Arsenal **1**
Hawley

v

Spurs **3**
Crooks 2, Hazard

This win at the home of anti-football goes a long way towards helping Spurs finish above Arsenal in the League for the first time since returning to the top flight in 1979. Keith Burkinshaw's exciting side are bringing the good times back to White Hart Lane, and briefly light up Highbury with their sunshine football.

61–0

World Class

When England won the World Cup in 1966 it was with former Spurs player Alf Ramsey at the helm. No Arsenal player has ever gone on to manage a World Cup-winning team.

Three England Lions

Three former Spurs players have gone on to manage England, all achieving notable success. Alf Ramsey, Terry Venables and Glenn Hoddle have all led the Three Lions with distinction. No Arsenal player has ever gone on to manage England.

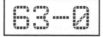

Heroes and Villains

Spurs are rightfully proud of the players and managers it has provided for England. The Gooners' most famous contribution to the national team is typically Arsenal.

The 1937 'Battle of Highbury' is infamous for being one of the dirtiest England internationals of all time. Italy centre back Luis Monti broke his foot in a crunching tackle after two minutes of a match littered with fouling and fighting. Stanley Matthews called it the most violent match of his career.

Seven of the 11 England players that day played for Arsenal.

64--0

Back to the Future

Fifty-two years later they were at it again. In 1989, Arsenal were fined £20,000 after a 21-man on-pitch brawl at Highbury against Norwich City, which the Police Federation labelled 'hooliganism'.

The following season they were deducted points after going toe-to-toe with Manchester United players at Old Trafford, prompting manager George Graham to say, 'Our disciplinary record is outstanding, apart from that Norwich thing last year.' Spurs players have never been labelled 'hooligans'.

65–0

Bunch of Fives

Monday 4 April 1983, White Hart Lane, Division One

Spurs **5**

Hughton 2, Brazil, Falco 2

v

Arsenal **0**

A scintillating socking from the super Spurs culminates in Mark Falco's scorching shoulder-high 20-yard volley on the run, one of the finest derby goals ever. After the game, Spurs fans serenade the Arsenal team bus off with chants of '5-0, 5-0, 5-0'. Legend has it that former Spurs hero Pat Jennings, now with Arsenal but dropped for the game, raises one of his enormous hands at the back window and, smiling, spreads five fingers wide.

Wembley's Wonder Goals

In a poll of football fans to find the best goals scored at the old Wembley Stadium, Spurs players took three of the top five spots:

1. Paul Gascoigne
England v Scotland, Euro 1996
Flick over Colin Hendry and slot.

2. Ricky Villa
Spurs v Man City, 1981 FA Cup Final
Mazy dribble through almost the entire
City team to score the winner.

5. Paul Gascoigne
Spurs v Arsenal, 1991 FA Cup semi-final
Thunderbolt from 200 yards.
No Arsenal players were anywhere in sight.

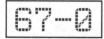

Myopia Wengeris

SPURS 5

ARSENAL 1

SEE THAT ARSENE?

A Google search for 'Arsène Wenger – I did not see the incident' throws up over 400,000 results, including offside goals, alleged elbows, clear-cut fouls and flying pizza. But after one derby match in 2008, it appeared that 20/20 vision had miraculously returned.

'We had 500 passes, Tottenham had 222; we had 18 shots on goal, Tottenham had 12; and we had 64 per cent of the possession,' said eagle-eyed Wenger. 'That sums up the game.' The one stat he forgot was Spurs' five goals to Arsenal's one. Perhaps he couldn't see the score on the Jumbotron (see 86-0).

V is for Victory

Tuesday 1 January 1985, Highbury, Division One

Arsenal **1**
Woodcock

v

Spurs **2**
Crooks, Falco

An 11.30 kick-off on New Year's Day sees scores of hungover, fancy-dress clad fans turn up straight from the previous night's parties to watch Spurs go top of the table with two late goals after Arsenal go one up.
Spurs outplay the hosts, and the great Graham Roberts delivers a heartfelt New Year message after Mark Falco's winner by flicking the Vs at the West Stand.

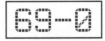

49
CLIVE ALLEN

44
TED DRAKE

In the 1986/87 season, Tottenham Hotspur's
Clive Allen scored 49 goals in all competitions.
Arsenal's top scorer in a single season was
Ted Drake, with 44 goals, in 1934/35.

70--0

Cake Walk

If you're feeling peckish and you're near a branch of Greggs the bakers you can always help yourself to a slice of Tottenham cake. The traditional sponge squares with pink icing on top were baked by local Quakers and handed out for free following the team's historic FA Cup win in 1901.

There are no sweet-tasting baked goods bearing the name of Arsenal available, not even just desserts.

Flat Champagne

Arsenal **0**

v

Spurs **0**

Even from a goalless draw, Spurs are capable
of fashioning legend, and Graham Roberts'
tackle on 'Champagne' Charlie Nicholas in this
New Year's Day fixture cements Robbo's place
in fan folklore.

The challenge is described by *The Times* as
having 'all the finesse of a charging rhino',
catapulting Nicholas off the pitch, through
advertising hoardings and into the arms of the
spectators in the stand. The chant of *Who Put
Charlie in the Stand?* is still sung to this day.

Player of the Year Awards

14

13

Tottenham Hotspur players have won the Football Writers' and PFA Player of the Year awards on 14 occasions. Arsenal players have been named 13 times. These awards have been won by eight different Spurs players, while seven different Arsenal players have secured the honours.

73–0

PAT JENNINGS

	Spurs	Arsenal
Appearances	591	327
FA Cups	1	1
League Cups	2	0
UEFA Cups	1	0
Goals	1	0

As any scientist will tell you, the way to compare any two variables is to introduce a constant. In the case of Spurs and Arsenal, that constant is Pat Jennings. Big Pat won four trophies at Spurs and famously scored in the FA Charity Shield against Man Utd. His time at Arsenal was less glorious. Despite playing in three successive FA Cup Finals, he only had one winner's medal to show for his time there.

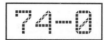

St Hotspur's Day

Sunday 14 April 1991, Wembley Stadium, FA Cup semi-final

Arsenal **1**
Smith

v

Spurs **3**
Lineker 2, Gascoigne

The ingredients for this first-ever FA Cup
semi-final at Wembley are mouth-watering:
Spurs stare bankruptcy in the face while red-
hot favourites Arsenal are chasing the Double.
Cue Gazza's wonder free-kick, backed up by
brilliant performances from a mercurial midfield
and heroic defence – and St Hotspur's Day is
complete. Arsenal's ambitions are spiked;
silky Spurs' future is secured.

Spiritual Home

For a club that's changed identities four times, it's no surprise that Arsenal has struggled to find a place to call 'home'. Born on Plumstead Common, they moved after one year to Plumstead Marshes, then the Manor Ground in Plumstead, and finally the Invicta Ground, before uprooting completely to go to Highbury, aka 'The Library'. In 2006 they realized that the best thing about their stadium was a clock, so they moved again. Determined not to lose all that history they'd built up, they named their new ground, um, The Emirates. Incredibly, they've managed to create somewhere even quieter than 'The Library', with 96 per cent of their supporters surveyed requesting a SECOND singing section.

It's all a far (and quiet) cry from White Hart Lane, a proper football stadium that has been synonymous with Spurs and a raucous atmosphere since 1899. As the *Bolton Evening News* put it: 'the best stage in the Premiership . . . the noise is constant and electric and the passion is tangible'.

First at the Last

Arsenal **1**
Dickov

v

Spurs **3**
Sheringham, Hendry 2

It's the Premier League's inaugural season and the annual battle for north London bragging rights has come down to the last match. Arsenal start the day in 9th, two places ahead of Spurs but only on goal difference. Golden Boot winner Teddy Sheringham opens the scoring before John Hendry makes sure Spurs end the day on top – and all in front of a gutted home support.

77–0

League Cup Wins

Both teams have reached the League Cup Final seven times, with Spurs getting their hands on the trophy four times and Arsenal picking up losers' medals in five of their finals.

78–0

The Glory Game

Hunter Davies' 1972 behind-the-scenes account of life at Spurs was hailed as the most insightful book about a football club ever published. It is still revered today as the best book ever written about the game.

Nick Hornby's romanticized account of following Arsenal through their 1989 title-fluking season, on the other hand, played a key part in the sanitization of the game and opened the door to a wave of 'born again' football fans. Even Arsenal fans hate *Fever Pitch* for making them look like they've got a sense of humour.

Fever Pitch

79–0

Beginning of the End

Sunday 7 November 1999, White Hart Lane, Premier League

Spurs **2**
Iversen, Sherwood

v

Arsenal **1**
Vieira

The Arsenal side of Vieira, Petit and Henry fancy their title chances, and are even more confident they can beat an ordinary Spurs side containing Tim Sherwood, Ruel Fox and Oyvind Leonhardsen. Yet after 19 minutes the Gooners are 2-0 down and blow their chances of a comeback when first Freddie Ljungberg and then Martin Keown are sent off. It's a victory that contributes to Arsenal finishing a massive 18 points behind champions Manchester United.

80--0

Filthy Arse

Think of 'rugged' players at Spurs and you might come up with Dave McKay, Graham Roberts and Pat Van Den Hauwe (very few others). But the names of dirty Arsenal players trip off the tongue: Frank McLintock, Willie Young, Nigel Winterburn, Tony Adams, Martin Keown, Ian Wright, Patrick Vieira, Mathieu Flamini, etc. When goalkeeper Wojciech Szczesny got red-carded against Bayern Munich in 2014, it was the 100th red card during Arsène Wenger's reign.

81—0

Anchormen

GARY LINEKER
MATCH OF THE DAY

BOB WILSON
FOOTBALL FOCUS

Both north London clubs have produced seasoned TV presenters. Arsenal's Wilson was always a safe pair of hands (apart from when he played in goal) but more of a substitute, coming on for the likes of Jimmy Hill and Des Lynam. Spurs' Lineker, on the other hand, has become the BBC's go-to anchor for the big occasion, including World Cups, Olympics and *Sports Personality of the Year*. And when it comes to their middle names, Gary Winston Lineker trumps Bob Primrose Wilson yet again.

82–0

Party Poopers

Saturday 22 April 2006, Highbury, Premier League

Arsenal **1**
Henry

v

Spurs **1**
Keane

In the last derby to be played at Highbury –
before the Woolwich Nomads move ground yet
again – Spurs give the hosts an uncomfortable
afternoon. After dominating the first half they
take the lead through Robbie Keane and it's not
until the 84th minute that substitute Thierry
Henry levels the scores to save the home side's
blushes. The party jellies are well and truly
wobbled and the pop left a bit flat.

Feeder Clubs

If you're going to be a feeder club, better to be one to Real Madrid (Gareth Bale, Luka Modric) than rival Manchester clubs (Robin Van Persie, Gael Clichy and Samir Nasri). Especially when you get a world record fee of £85m (even if you do subsequently piss it up the wall).

Parks' Life

Tony Parks, goalkeeping hero of the 1984 UEFA Cup Final penalty shootout, grew up in north London in the 1970s as an Arsenal fan in a family of Arsenal supporters. But, as he said in the book *The Boys from White Hart Lane*, 'The day I walked into Tottenham I was a real convert. Tottenham was the club I loved as a footballer.'

85–0

A Thrashing and a Punch-Up

Tuesday 22 January 2008, White Hart Lane,
Carling Cup semi-final 2nd leg

Spurs **5**

Jenas, Bendtner og, Keane, Lennon, Malbranque

v

Arsenal **1**

Adebayor

Spurs haven't beaten Arsenal for nine years, but
Arsène Wenger is still worried enough to field
seven first team regulars. Spurs rip into the visitors
from the off, taking an early lead, then going 2-1
up thanks to an own goal, and finally running
Arsenal ragged. To cap it all, Nicklas Bendtner and
Emmanuel Adebayor come to blows on the pitch.
Wenger tries to play down the 5-1 defeat (6-1 on
aggregate), saying: 'We have priorities that are
much more important than the Carling Cup.'
Priorities like the FA Cup (out in round five), the
Champions League (out in the quarters) and the
Premiership (third place)?
Spurs go on to win the final 2-1 against Chelsea.

Tight Arse

Seeing Arsenal defensive coach Steve Bould poncing about in his 'budgie-smuggler' tight white shorts is a painful reminder of what Arsenal players wore with pleasure in the mid to late 80s. Thankfully, Spurs had the balls to correct this footballing fashion faux pas, introducing baggier, longer shorts for their 1991 FA Cup Final victory – a winning style that was soon followed by all clubs. Including Arsenal.

87–0

Famous Fans

SPURS	ARSENAL
Kenneth Branagh *(Henry V)*	Tom Watt *(Lofty)*
Trevor McDonald *(Sir)*	Dermot Murnaghan *(Mr)*
Michael Holding *(249 Test wickets)*	Phil Tufnell *(121 Test wickets)*
Pierce Brosnan *(007)*	Piers Morgan *(zero)*
Bob Marley *(Wailer)*	Dido *(wailer)*
Salman Rushdie *(Booker Prize)*	Nick Hornby *(William Hill Sports Book of the Year)*
Peter Cook *(funny)*	Rory McGrath *(not funny)*

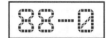

Top Draw

Arsenal **4**
Silvestre, Gallas, Adebayor, Van Persie

v

Spurs **4**
Bentley, Bent, Jenas, Lennon

Spurs are bottom of the table, bereft of hope,
a shambles, and 4-2 down with one minute
remaining. Then Jermaine Jenas curls a beauty
past Manuel Almunia and, with 10 seconds to go,
Aaron Lennon prods home the equalizer.
Cue pandemonium in the away end and silence in
the home sections. Stunned silence, that is, not
the usual Emirates kind.

Club Philosophers

*'I have been here before as a spirit –
this is just my physical body, it is just
an overcoat. And at death, you will
take the overcoat off.'*

GLENN HODDLE

'I saw Kiss Me Kate *with the
mother-in-law. I'm going to see the
film version of* Les Mis *next week.
I walk the dog. That enough?'*

TONY ADAMS

Goal Machines

200+

Two Spurs players have bagged more than
200 goals for the club – Jimmy Greaves with
266 and Bobby Smith with 208.
Only one player, Thierry Henry, has broken
the 200 barrier for Arsenal.

Twice as Nice

Spurs **2**
Rose, Bale

v

Arsenal **1**
Bendtner

It's the business end of the season, with
Arsenal looking to win the Premier League
and Spurs aiming for the Champions League.
Debutant Danny Rose's early wonder-volley
sends the decibel counter off the scale and
Gareth Bale turns the volume up further soon
after half-time. Spurs dominate and Bendtner's
late strike is no more than a consolation.
It's a doubly sweet victory, helping to kill off
Arsenal's title challenge while propelling
Spurs towards the Champions League.

Bad Hair Days

Arsenal have been guilty of some of the most heinous hair crimes against football, including Alan Sunderland's afro and 'tache combo, Ray Parlour's ginger perm, David Seaman's porn-star ponytail and Freddie Ljungberg's pink Mohican. It's true that Ljungberg became a knickers model, but only one north London footballer's barnet has been deemed 'worth it' by hair experts L'Oreal – step forward, Spurs midfield maestro and shampoo seller extraordinaire, Monsieur David Ginola.

93–0

The Rudest Football Chant Ever

The Spurs/Arsenal rivalry has given rise to
some classic songs, with Spurs fans credited
for arguably the most unique and most sweary
football chant of all time.

'My old man said be an Arsenal fan,
I said f*** off, b******s you're a c***.'

94-0

Turnaround Titans

Saturday 20 November 2010, Emirates Stadium,
Premier League

Arsenal **2**
Nasri, Chamakh

v

Spurs **3**
Bale, Van der Vaart, Kaboul

After just 27 minutes Spurs are fearing the worst
when Arsenal cruise to a two-goal lead. Spurs
get to half-time without further damage, after
which a typical piece of wizardry from Gareth
Bale and a cool penalty from Dutch Master
Rafa Van der Vaart set up a final 20 minutes of
all-out attack. Then, with five minutes to go,
Younes Kaboul rises to head home and pull off a
stunning and victorious comeback.

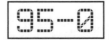

Anagram-a-ding-dong II

(The Emirates)

Vorsprung Durch Technik

JÜRGEN KLINNSMANN
29 goals (1994/95 season)

MESUT ÖZIL
7 goals (2013/14 season)

When it comes to buying a flashy German import, Spurs race away with this one. Spurs' German international cost only £2m, and in Klinsmann's first season he scored 29 goals and won the Football Writers' Footballer of the Year. Being at a club like Spurs allowed Klinsmann's skill as well as sense of humour to flourish, endearing himself to a previously sceptical English football public.

Özil's transfer to Arsenal has been less of a German fairytale. Arsène Wenger was bullied by fans into spending the money he'd been hoarding, splashing out a ridiculous £42.5m on a player whose performances in an Arsenal shirt went steadily downhill and resulted in only seven goals.

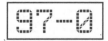
97--0

10,000 Up

Sunday 2 October 2011, White Hart Lane, Premier League

Spurs **2**
Van der Vaart, Walker

v

Arsenal **1**
Ramsey

Arsenal are languishing in the wrong half of the table and it's Spurs' chance to put the boot in. Rafa Van der Vaart opens the scoring with Spurs' 10,000th goal in all competitions and Kyle Walker fires home a late long-range winner. At the final whistle Arsenal are 15th in the table, London's lowliest club.

The win strips away Arsenal's façade of superiority and, in the words of the *Telegraph*'s Henry Winter, leaves the club 'so far back, it is like finding Joan Collins in Economy'.

The Whiff of Decay

When Arsenal laid the North Bank foundations in 1913, locals were asked to dump their rubbish to help build up the terrace. Legend has it that a local coal merchant backed his pony and trap too close to the hole and lost them both into the pit.

Arsenal's affinity for refuse continued when they moved to the new Emirates Stadium in the early 21st century, selecting a site on top of an old municipal dump.

White Hart Lane was built on the fragrant site of a former nursery.

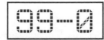

First

1882
1886

In the final analysis, the unchallengeable facts are that whatever Arsenal have achieved, Spurs beat them to it – Spurs were formed first, won the FA Cup first, won the League Cup first, won the Double first and won a European trophy first.

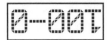

17

28

Major Trophies

Fever Pitch

Is it any wonder that the most
celebrated football book ever
is about being an Arsenal fan?

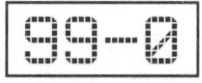

Three in a Row

Arsenal jointly hold the record for the most consecutive League titles won. The Gunners' hat-trick came in 1933, 1934 and 1935. In the space of three years, Arsenal won more titles than Spurs have in their entire history.

Head-to-Head, *Part II*

Not only do Arsenal have a superior win
percentage in north London derbies, the Gunners
also have a better head-to-head record against
Spurs in every major competition they've played:
the League, FA Cup and League Cup.

97-0

The Double

1971, 1998, 2002

1961

Spurs have set some records; in 1961 they became the first team to win the League and FA Cup double, which was nice for them. Arsenal have achieved it three times since.

Cheeky Treble

Sunday 16 March 2014, White Hart Lane, Premier League

Spurs **0**

v

Arsenal **1**

Rosicky

On the face of it, this looks like another routine
Arsenal 1-0 win at Spurs – Tomas Rosicky scores
after two minutes and it's job done.
But this derby win tastes a little sweeter
because it means Arsenal have done a treble
over Spurs in the 2013/14 season, having already
beaten them twice at The Emirates; 1-0 in the
Premier League and 2-0 in the FA Cup.

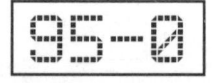

Legend Count

17

Alf Common
Charles Buchan
David Jack
Alex James
Eddie Hapgood
Cliff Bastin
Wilf Copping
Ted Drake
Joe Mercer
Tommy Lawton
Frank McLintock
Pat Jennings
Alan Ball
Malcolm Macdonald
Liam Brady
Tony Adams
Dennis Bergkamp

14

Viv Woodward
Alf Ramsey
Danny Blanchflower
Cliff Jones
Jimmy Greaves
Dave Mackay
Alan Mullery
Martin Peters
Pat Jennings
Ossie Ardiles
Ray Clemence
Glenn Hoddle
Gary Lineker
Paul Gascoigne

When the Football League unveiled a list of 100 legends as part of its centenary celebrations in 1998, there were 17 players from Arsenal and 14 from Spurs.

Famous Fans

ARSENAL

SPURS

Roger Daltrey *(Who)*	V	**Andrew Ridgeley** *(who?)*
Fidel Castro *(50 years)*	V	**Iain Duncan Smith** *(23 months)*
Robert Peston *(clear)*	V	**Michael Fish** *(foggy)*
Matt Lucas *(yeah but, no but)*	V	**Michael McIntyre** *(no)*
Melvyn Bragg *(quality)*	V	**Richard Littlejohn** *(tabloid)*
Mick Jagger *(front man)*	V	**Phil Collins** *(drummer)*
Sam Fox *(DD)*	V	**Linda Lusardi** *(D)*

Box-to-Box

Highbury
HENRY COOPER
V
MUHAMMED ALI
1966

White Hart Lane
MICHAEL WATSON
V
CHRIS EUBANK
1991

Both clubs' grounds have hosted boxing bouts in
the past, but only one hosted The Greatest.

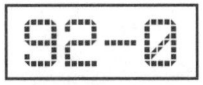

Lightning Strikes Twice

Saturday 17 November 2012, Emirates Stadium, Premier League

Arsenal **5**

Mertesacker, Podolski, Giroud, Cazorla, Walcott

v

Spurs **2**

Adebayor, Bale

Nine months on, and once again Spurs fans
believe they have the team to finally finish above
Arsenal in the table.
Again Spurs take the lead, but then that nice
chap Emmanuel Adebayor gets himself sent off
and the Gunners blitz them once again. Theo
Walcott adds the fifth in the last minute to
match the score from the previous season.

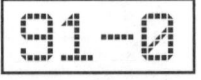

The Battle of Highbury

Funnily enough, the match known as 'The Battle of Highbury' wasn't a north London derby. It was an international between England and Italy in 1934 that was particularly dirty. What's notable about it from a north London perspective is that Arsenal provided a record seven starting players to the England team (Spurs provided none).
Arsenal (sorry, England) beat the World Cup holders 3-2.

90-0

Mind the Gap

Sunday 26 February 2012, Emirates Stadium, Premier League

Arsenal **5**

Sagna, Van Persie, Rosicky, Walcott (2)

Spurs **2**

Saha, Adebayor

Arsenal go into the match 10 points behind Spurs in the chase for a top-four place and are shocked to be 2-0 down after 34 minutes. Is this going to be the moment that Spurs finally manage to emerge from their shadow after 15 years of always finishing second best? Er, no. Bacary Sagna starts the fightback and Theo Walcott finishes it off with a brace to cap a memorable comeback win.

What might have been a 13-point gap in the League becomes seven points and Spurs crumble in the run-in as Arsenal overhaul them again.

Head-to-Head

You'll have worked it out by now – Arsenal are just better at football than Spurs.

Played 177

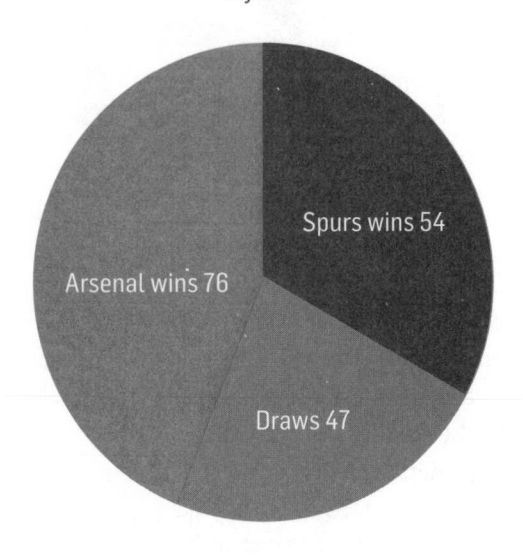

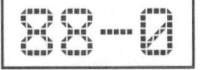

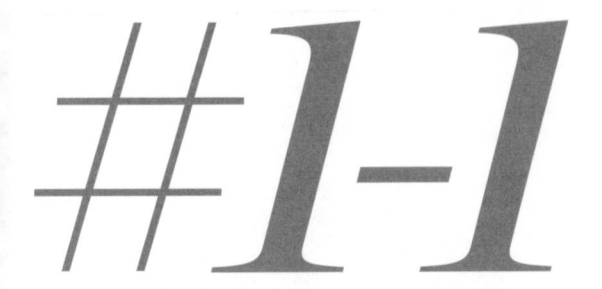

Last day of the 2012/13 season, and Spurs need to get a better result than Arsenal to clinch fourth place and a spot in the Champions League. Both are playing tight games and lead 1-0, when former Spurs chairman Alan Sugar tweets that Newcastle have equalized against Arsenal. '1-1 at Newcastle,' he says, and thousands of Spurs fans celebrate as if it's too good to be true. It is too good to be true.

Sugar has got it wrong and Spurs miss out again as Arsenal hold on for the 1-0 win. Sweet.

87-0

Social Club

@

Arsenal have millions more 'likes' on Facebook
than Spurs. Similarly on Twitter, @Arsenal has
millions more followers than @SpursOfficial.
Even in cyberspace Arsenal are winning.
#biggerclub

Dennis Does the Double

Goal of the Season was started by *Match of the Day* in 1970/71 and Arsenal have won it four times.

You've just been reminded of the Henry and Adebayor classics. Arsenal's two others were scored by Dennis Bergkamp. First, against Leicester in 1997, from a month where he became the only player to ever get first, second and third in Goal of the Month. His second Goal of the Season was the miracle spin-and-finish against Newcastle in 2002.

Spurs have managed Goal of the Season just once.

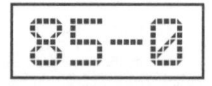

Goal of the Season, *Part II*

Saturday 15 September 2007, White Hart Lane, Premier League

Spurs **1**
Bale

v

Arsenal **3**
Adebayor (2), Fabregas

Arsenal fans don't think fondly of Emmanuel
Adebayor, but he had a nice habit of scoring
against Spurs in the north London derby.
His second in this match is a peach – he flicks
the ball up on the edge of the box with one
touch, and spins and volleys it into the corner
with the next.
Victory at White Hart Lane and Goal of the
Season to Adebayor.

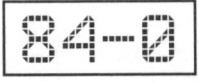

Neighbourhood Watch

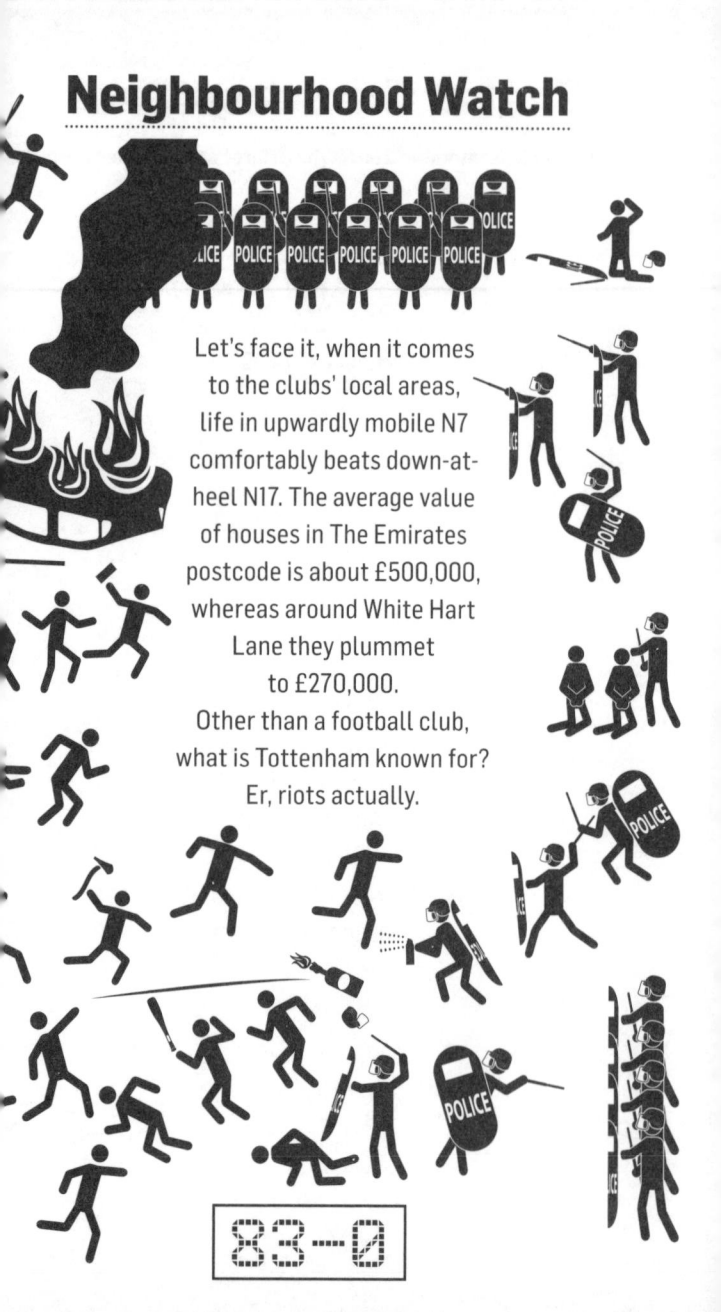

Let's face it, when it comes to the clubs' local areas, life in upwardly mobile N7 comfortably beats down-at-heel N17. The average value of houses in The Emirates postcode is about £500,000, whereas around White Hart Lane they plummet to £270,000. Other than a football club, what is Tottenham known for? Er, riots actually.

Going Underground

The Gunners have made such an impression on their local area that they even changed the name of the Tube station to Arsenal. Tottenham doesn't even have a Tube station.

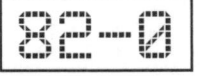

The Home of Football

'Happy those
who can
remain at
Highbury.'

JANE AUSTEN, *EMMA*.

There is no known classical literary reference
to White Hart Lane for some reason.

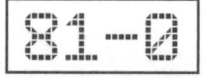

The Kids Are Alright

Wednesday 31 January 2007, The Emirates,
League Cup semi-final second leg

Arsenal **3**
Adebayor, Aliadière, Rosicky

v

Spurs **1**
Mido

Seven days later and the humiliation of Spurs'
first team at the hands of the Arsenal kids is
complete. The crucial moment comes when
Spurs defender Riccardo Rocha decides he'll
try to head away a cross from Justin Hoyte,
but by the time the ball reaches him it's no
more than two inches off the ground.
Like Spurs, Rocha falls flat on his face, and
his attempted clearance drops straight to
Jeremie Aliadière, who promptly scores
Arsenal's crucial second.

Low Grade

v Arsenal

- ☑ CATEGORY A
- ☐ CATEGORY B
- ☐ CATEGORY C

For the 2007 League Cup semi-final first leg at White Hart Lane, Spurs rated the match Category A. Arsenal were less excited by the opposition for the return leg, classing the game at The Emirates a Category B.

v Spurs

- ☐ CATEGORY A
- ☑ CATEGORY B
- ☐ CATEGORY C

79–0

Musical Tributes

TONY ADAMS
by Joe Strummer

OSSIE'S DREAM
by Chas & Dave

78-0

Nuclear Sub

He's not going to go down as a Gunners legend,
but here's another Arsenal goal-scoring record
for you. The fastest goal ever scored by a
substitute in the Premier League was by Nicklas
Bendtner in 2007, heading home the winner in a
2-1 victory 1.8 seconds after coming on. And who
was it against? Spurs.

1.8

Nice One, Sir Henry

Arsenal

Arsenal

Before competitive football resumed after the
First World War, the Football League decided to
expand the First Division from 20 teams to 22.
The plan was to keep the two teams that had
been relegated in 1914/15, but Arsenal chairman
Henry Norris pointed out that the 1914/15
season had been rife with match-fixing, and
cannily persuaded the League to hold a ballot.
It was a ballot that Arsenal won, so despite
finishing fifth in the Second Division in 1915, the
Gunners gained promotion to the top flight.
And who was the only team to be relegated
from the First Division in such unfortunate
and murky circumstances? Why, Tottenham
Hotspur of course.

Arsenal

Arsenal

senal

```
76-0
```

Regular Fixture

While Tottenham have yo-yoed between the First and Second Division several times, Arsenal are the top flight's longest serving team, with an unbroken run since 1919. And there's a funny story about how that came about . . .

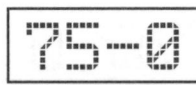

75—0

'2-0 and You F***ed it Up!'

Wednesday 24 January 2007, White Hart Lane,
League Cup semi-final first leg

Spurs **2**
Berbatov, Baptista (og)

v

Arsenal **2**
Baptista (2)

Arsène Wenger's policy over the years has
been to play predominantly a youth team in
the League Cup campaign, and even when
Arsenal draw Spurs in the semi-final he
sticks to his guns.
Spurs lead 2-0 midway through the second
half, but Alex Hleb comes on to add a little
bit of extra know-how and the Gunners' kids
show that even they are a match for Spurs'
first team.

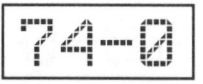

Club Crest

Ours is a gun,
theirs is a chicken.

Arsenal Win the
World Cup Again

Twelve years after Emmanuel Petit and
Patrick Vieira won the World Cup with
France, Arsenal's Cesc Fabregas played
a key role in Spain's triumph, setting up
Andrés Iniesta for the winning goal in the
2010 World Cup Final.
No player has ever won a World Cup Final
while representing Spurs.

Biggest Win

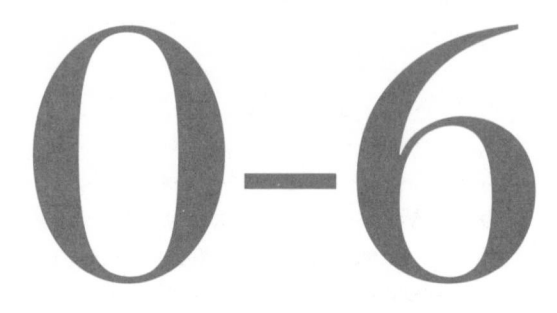

The biggest margin of victory in a north London derby is a thumping 6-0 win for the Gunners at White Hart Lane in Division One in 1935.

71–0

Arsenal Win the World Cup

After winning the double in 1998,
Emmanuel Petit and Patrick Vieira went
on to win the World Cup with France, with
Vieira setting up Petit for the third goal in
the 3-0 win over Brazil in the final.
'Arsenal win the World Cup' was the
Mirror's headline.
No player has ever won a World Cup Final
while representing Spurs.

70--0

Spurs Swamped

Saturday 13 November 2004, White Hart Lane, Premier League

Spurs **4**
Naybet, Defoe, King, Kanouté

v

Arsenal **5**
Henry, Lauren, Vieira, Ljungberg, Pires

It takes a special kind of team to score four goals at home and still lose.
This match is the highest scoring north London derby of all time. And when it's raining goals in a derby, you can bet your life that Spurs will be on the receiving end.
Arsenal's big guns are irresistible on the day, with sublime finishes from Vieira, Ljungberg and Pires. Late King and Kanouté goals aren't enough to stop the red tide and prevent Spurs from drowning.

They Managed Both Sides

TERRY NEILL

Like George Graham, Terry Neill is another who has managed both Arsenal and Spurs. Unlike Graham, Neill went from Spurs to Arsenal – but of course the result was the same. Neill enjoyed success at Highbury, guiding the Gunners to three consecutive FA Cup Finals and winning the famous trophy in 1979. He won nothing at Spurs.

68–0

Pony and Trap

On the subject of kits, is it any coincidence
that for a number of seasons Spurs' kit
manufacturer was Pony? Pony is, of course,
Cockney rhyming slang for . . . well, if you don't
know already, you can look it up.

Better Red

LIVERPOOL 021	**SPAIN** 1835	**MAN UNITED** 945
ROMA 296	**BAYERN** 0455	**AC MILAN** 3365
ARSENAL 1775	**AJAX** 025	**BENFICA** 1812

A university study a few years back determined
that success has a colour, and that colour is red.
Teams that wear red win more games than teams
wearing any other colour.

Home Advantage?

WHITE HART LANE N17

TOTTENHAM HOTSPUR FOOTBALL CLUB

So that means Arsenal have won the league at White Hart Lane as many times as Spurs have.

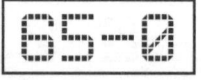

'Seventy One,
Two Thousand and Four'

Sunday 25 April 2004, White Hart Lane, Premier League

Spurs **2**
Redknapp, Keane

v

Arsenal **2**
Vieira, Pires

Winning the league at White Hart Lane is so
enjoyable that Arsenal decide to do it again.
Once more a draw is good enough to give the
Gunners the title, and Patrick Vieira and Robert
Pires score in the first half to ensure it's never
in doubt. Even a last-minute equalizer doesn't
dampen the celebrations as Arsenal rub their
superiority in Spurs' faces.

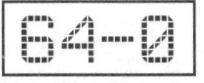

When the Year Ends in 1, 2, 3, 4, 5, 6, 7, 8, 9 or 0

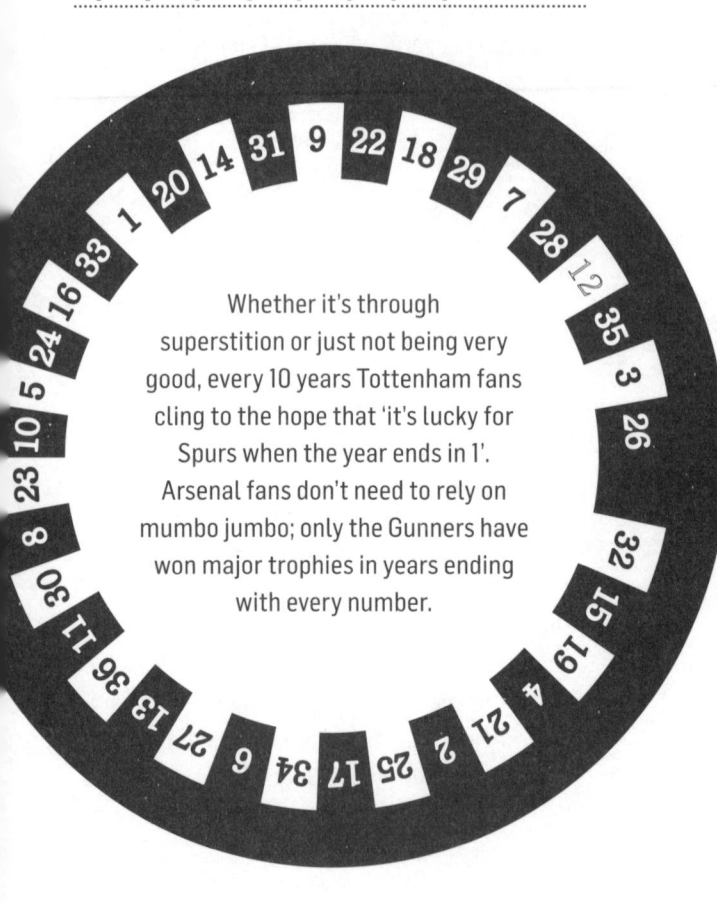

Whether it's through superstition or just not being very good, every 10 years Tottenham fans cling to the hope that 'it's lucky for Spurs when the year ends in 1'. Arsenal fans don't need to rely on mumbo jumbo; only the Gunners have won major trophies in years ending with every number.

63–0

Derby Streaks

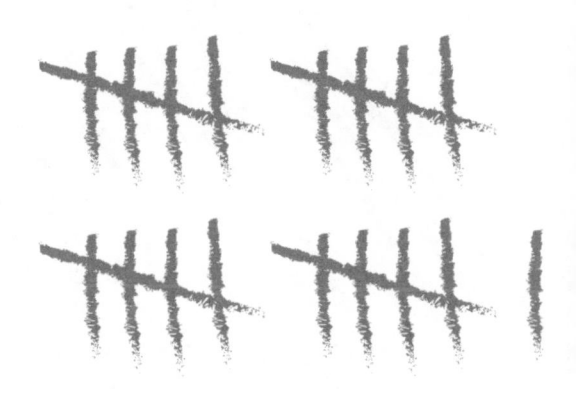

Starting with a 2-1 victory in March 2000 and running until January 2008, Arsenal went 21 games and nearly eight years unbeaten against Spurs. Spurs' best unbeaten streak against Arsenal was eight games in the mid-1940s.

Own Goal

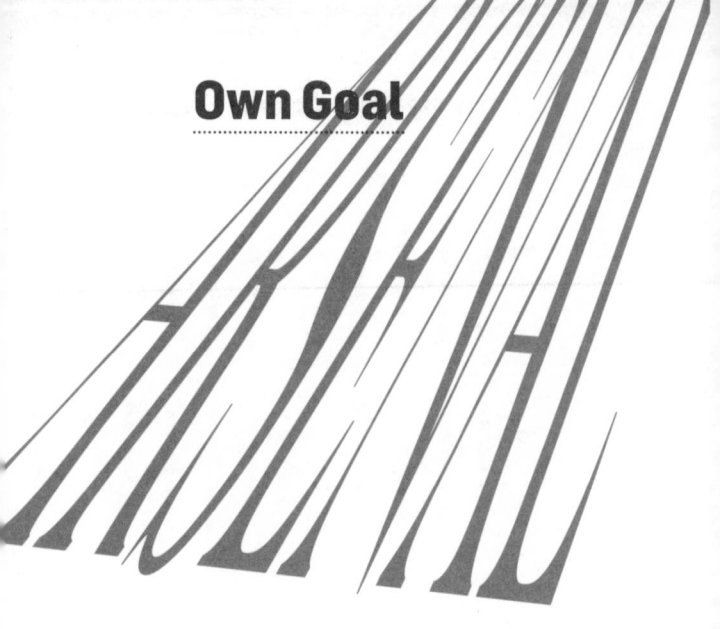

'In the early 1960s, Spurs had a great manager and a great team.
But they have never been a great club.
Even when we had Bill Nicholson as manager and the likes of Dave Mackay, Cliff Jones, Danny Blanchflower and myself, Spurs still lived in the shadow of Arsenal.'

**JIMMY GREAVES,
SPURS' LEADING GOALSCORER OF ALL TIME**

61 — 0

Team of the Century

1901 1977
1946 1969
1923
930 1908 1966 1989

Based on average finishing position in the league over the whole of the 20th century, from 1900 to 1999, Arsenal are the number one team in England – the true 'team of the century'.
Spurs are down in 6th.
Actually, that's not bad for a Cup team.

947

998

1966 1935 1992
1984 1918
1904
981 1952 197
1971 1907 1999

60–0

Goal of the Season, *Part I*

Saturday 16 November 2002, Highbury, Premier League

Arsenel **3**
Henry, Ljungberg, Wiltord

v

Spurs **0**

A 3-0 win in which Thierry Henry's wonder strike is voted Goal of the Season, and the fact that it's against Spurs makes it all the sweeter. Henry picks the ball up midway inside Arsenal's half, accelerates away from the Spurs midfield, ghosts past two more Spurs players, before passing the ball into the corner of the net with his left foot.

His iconic knee-sliding goal celebration in front of the Spurs fans is now immortalized outside the Emirates.

Epic Arsenal

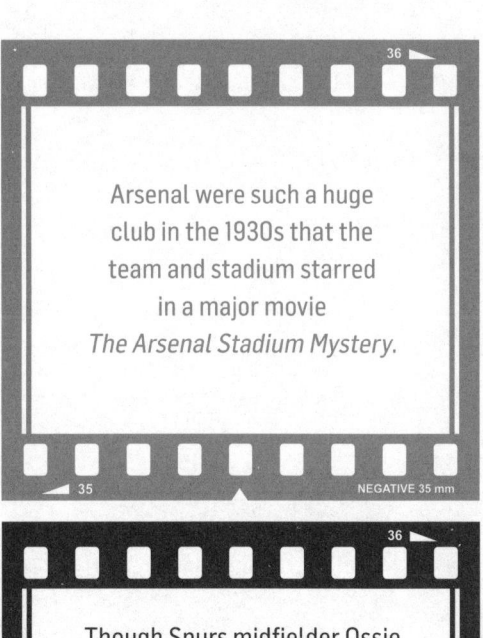

Arsenal were such a huge club in the 1930s that the team and stadium starred in a major movie *The Arsenal Stadium Mystery*.

36

35   NEGATIVE 35 mm

Though Spurs midfielder Ossie Ardiles was in *Escape to Victory* – where again he found himself playing alongside a cast of overpaid prima donnas – a film has never been made about Spurs or White Hart Lane.

36

35   NEGATIVE 35 mm

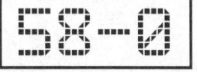

58–0

Black and White

Seeing as we're talking about early football coverage, it's probably a good time to point out that the only footage you'll see of a Spurs title-winning side will be filmed in black and white.

Media Darlings

In fact, Arsenal were chosen for the first match broadcast live on radio, the first match broadcast live on TV, the first *Match of the Day*, and the first match broadcast live in 3D.

Match of the Day

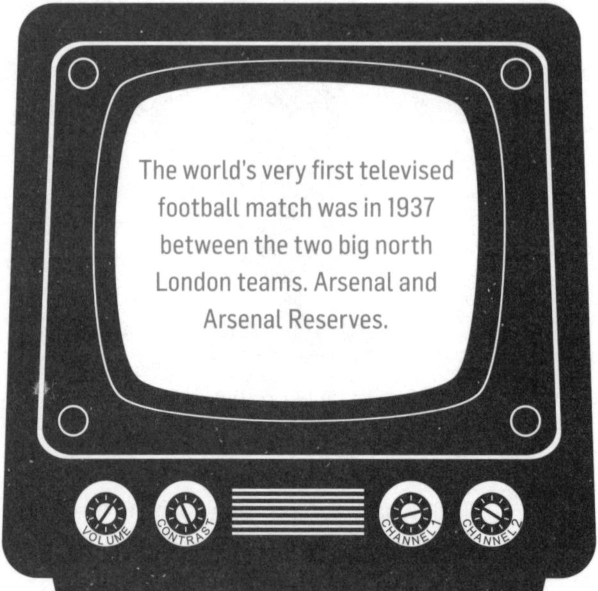

The world's very first televised football match was in 1937 between the two big north London teams. Arsenal and Arsenal Reserves.

55-0

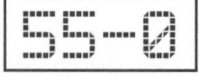

They Played for Both Sides

SOL
CAMPBELL

Let's face it, when your captain decides he wants
to walk out on you and join your most bitter rivals,
you've not got much going for you as a club.
Step forward, Sulzeer Jeremiah Campbell.
Campbell came to Arsenal 'to win trophies' and
won twice as many in his first season with the
Gunners as he did in nine seasons with Spurs.

54-0

Sol Sees the Light

Arsenal 2
Vieira, Pires

v

Spurs 1
Doherty

The scoreline doesn't do justice to Arsenal's performance as they dominate the match entirely. Captain of Spurs, in what turned out to be his last game for the club, was a certain Sol Campbell.
Maybe this was the moment that he saw the light?

53–0

Manager of the Year

Arsène Wenger has twice been voted manager of the year (2002, 2004). That's twice more than all the Spurs managers put together.

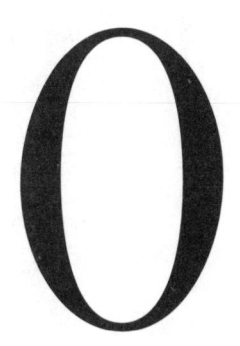

Bossing it

Arsène Wenger **v**

- Gerry Francis
- Chris Hughton *(caretaker)*
- Christian Gross
- David Pleat *(caretaker)*
- George Graham
- David Pleat *(caretaker)*
- Glenn Hoddle
- David Pleat *(caretaker)*
- Jacques Santini
- Martin Jol
- Clive Allen *(caretaker)*
- Juande Ramos
- Harry Redknapp
- André Villas-Boas
- Tim Sherwood
- Mauricio Pochettino
- Insert new manager here

51–0

Mind Games

'The difference this year is that we are on an upward spiral in terms of confidence, whereas they are in a negative spiral and once you get into that negative spiral it's difficult to get out of it.'

ANDRÉ VILLAS-BOAS, 3 MARCH 2013.

In little over two months Arsenal again leapfrog Spurs to fourth place and Villas-Boas is sacked before the year is out.

The Cup Double

1993

In 1993 Arsenal became the first club to complete a League Cup and FA Cup double, beating Sheffield Wednesday in both Wembley finals. Despite their reputation for being a cup team, Spurs have never achieved the domestic cup double.

Captain Fantastic

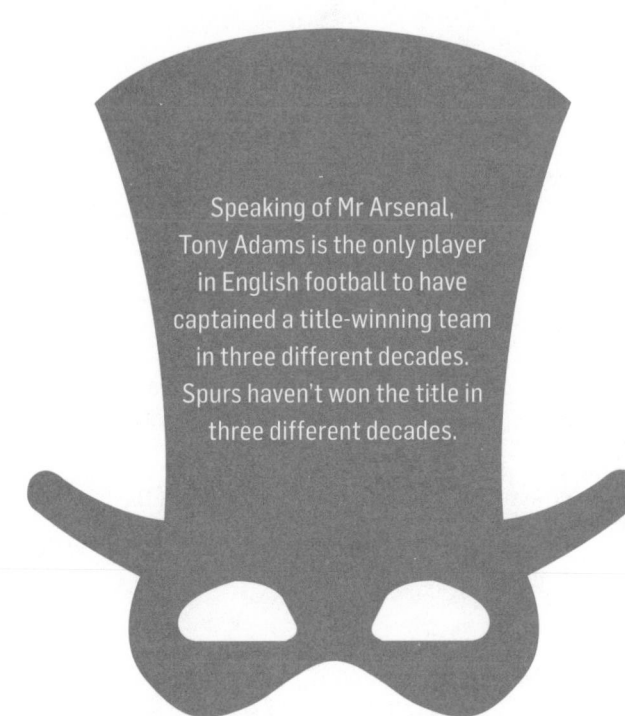

Speaking of Mr Arsenal, Tony Adams is the only player in English football to have captained a title-winning team in three different decades. Spurs haven't won the title in three different decades.

48–0

The Donkey Won the Derby

Sunday 4 April 1993, Wembley, FA Cup semi-final

Arsenal 1
Adams

v

Spurs 0

It's the second FA Cup semi-final between the two clubs, with Arsenal seeking revenge for the surprise defeat at Wembley in 1991.
Mr Arsenal himself, Tony Adams, rises at the far post to head home a late winner for a classic 1-0 win to the Arsenal. Right in so many ways.

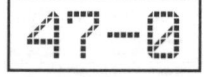

Money Well Spent

'We do not buy superstars, we make them.'

Arsène Wenger

Spurs don't buy superstars either. They swiftly splurged the Bale £85m and more on Eric Lamela (£30m), Roberto Soldado (£26m), Paulinho (£17m), Christian Eriksen (£11m), Etienne Capoué (£9m), Vlad Chiriches (£8.5m) and Nacer Chadli (£7m).

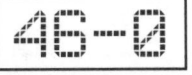

46—0

Bale out, Özil in

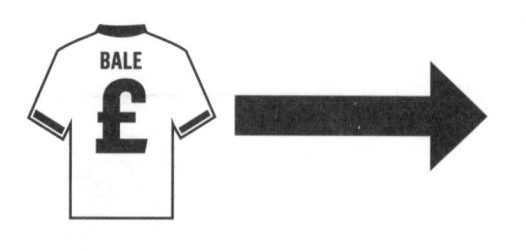

The most recent of those record transfers out of White Hart Lane was Gareth Bale to Real Madrid in 2013. And what was the upshot of that? Other than Spurs having even more money to waste, it meant that Madrid let Arsenal take Mesut Özil off their hands.

As the song goes, 'How does it feel to be Tottenham, how does it feel to be small? You sold Bale and we bought Mesut Özil.'

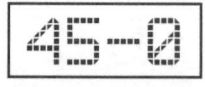

Selling Club

Of course, money's only good if you know
what to do with it. Four times in Arsenal's
history have they broken the British record
for the most expensive transfer.
Spurs have been involved in four British
record deals themselves, but in three of
them they were the selling club.

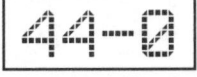

Even More Money

£15.3 BILLION

Arsenal

The combined wealth of Arsenal's major shareholders is estimated to be £15.3billion. Spurs can muster a mere £1.9billion. Chicken feed, really.

£1.9BILLION

Tottenham Hotspur

43–0

Share and Share Alike

£15,000
ARSENAL

While we're on the subject of money, to buy a share in Arsenal will cost you around £15,000. When Spurs delisted their shares in 2012, a share cost less than a packet of peanuts.

40p
TOTTENHAM HOTSPUR

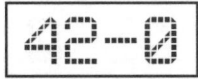

Money, Money, Money

$1.331
BILLION
Arsenal

$514
MILLION
Tottenham Hotspur

In the 2014 Forbes rankings of the most valuable football clubs, Spurs are eight places and $817m behind the world's fifth most valuable outfit – Arsenal.

41–0

Spurs Socked

Spurs **2**
Waddle, Gascoigne

v

Arsenal **3**
Winterburn, Marwood, Smith

One of the games in the late-80s winning streak is at the Lane in 1988. Don't let anyone tell you that Arsenal's defenders only learnt how to play expansive football under Arsène Wenger; the most memorable moment of this match is Tony Adams going on a mazy run in the Spurs half, dummying an opposing player before slipping Nigel Winterburn in to score a brilliant opener. Spurs' only highlight is Gazza scoring with his sock.

All five goals come in a madcap 12 minutes, sealing crucial points in the season when Arsenal win the League at Anfield with Michael Thomas's last-gasp goal.

Consecutive Derby Wins

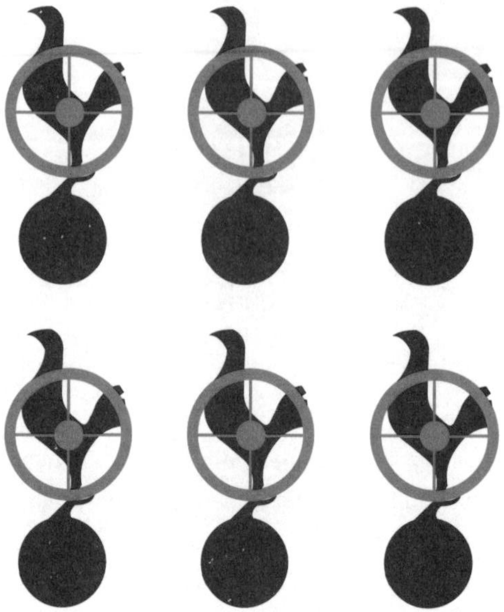

The longest winning streak in the history of
the north London derby is six. And which team
managed that six-game streak? The answer is
Arsenal. Twice.
First between 1977 and 1980 and then again
between 1987 and 1989.

13

2002

11

1961

Spurs once held the record for the most consecutive wins in a season in the top flight – they won 11 matches on the spin in 1961. They held that record until the end of the 2001/02 season, when it was broken and extended to 13 by . . . Arsenal.

'She Wore a Pair of Stockings'

Who knows what sort of success Spurs might have had if the reign of David Pleat hadn't been cut short? Unless you're currently drawing your pension, Pleat's team of the late 80s is probably the best Spurs team in living memory (they still didn't win the League of course). Sadly his employment as manager of Tottenham came to an end in October 1987 when he was dismissed due to 'disclosures about his private life'. And so the song went: '. . . and when I asked her why she wore those stockings, she said they're for my client and his name is David Pleat . . .'

37-0

Diamond Lights

**HEARING PROTECTION
MUST BE WORN**

Sorry for having to remind you of *Diamond Lights*
by 'Glenn & Chris', but this was a victory to Arsenal
without even having to get out of bed.

This dirge of a record was intended to cash in on a
freakishly good season for Spurs, culminating in a
third place League finish (the last time they made
the top three).

But in typical Spurs style, things had gone pear-
shaped with a League Cup semi-final exit at the
hands of Arsenal, a humbling FA Cup Final defeat,
plus revelations that manager David Pleat had been
charged three times by police for kerb-crawling.
Only one north London team were on song in 1987,
and that was League Cup winners Arsenal.

Hairy Moments

The 80s was an ugly decade for hair, with barber-shop casualties on both sides of the north London divide.
Glenn Hoddle and Paul Walsh had prize-winning mullets for Spurs, while Paul Mariner and Charlie Nicholas deserve special praise for Arsenal. There was one player, however, who over four seasons consistently let the Spurs team down, guaranteeing Arsenal victory in the style stakes. Sporting a ghastly array of mullets that could only look trendy in a sausage factory, step forward Chris Waddle.

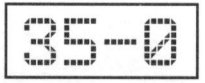

1-2 1-2 1-2 1-2

1-2 1-2
1-2 1-2

Within one calendar year – 1987 – Arsenal won four times at White Hart Lane, all by the same 1-2 scoreline. First in the League (January), then twice in the League Cup semi-final (March) and then again in the following League campaign (October). The song 'Can we play you every week?' was never more apt.

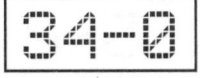

34-0

Longest Unbeaten
Run in a Season

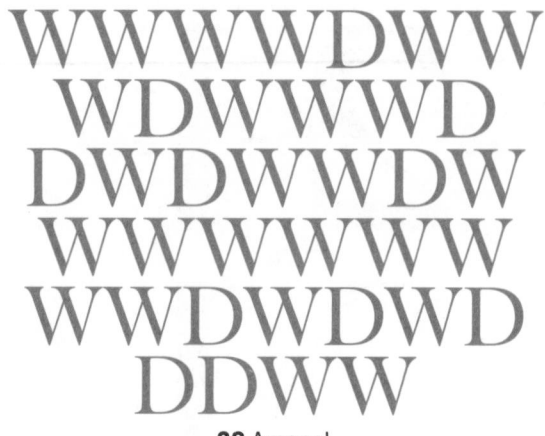

WWWWDWW
WDWWWD
DWDWWDW
WWWWWWW
WWDWDWD
DDWW

38 Arsenal

WWWWWWW
WDWDWWWW
WWWDWWDW

22 Spurs

Arsenal won the 2003/04 Premier League without being beaten during the entire 38-game campaign, earning the nickname 'The Invincibles'. Spurs' longest unbeaten run in a season was 22 matches, back in 1949 in Division Two.

33–0

FA Youth Cups

It's not just senior football where Arsenal put Spurs to shame. Arsenal have won 7 FA Youth Cups to Spurs' 3.

Ladies First

Arsenal Ladies are the most successful
team in English women's football history,
with 40 trophies and counting.
Spurs Ladies have never won a major trophy
in their history.

31—0

GEORGE GRAHAM
BILL NICHOLSON

Spurs' Bill Nicholson and Arsenal's George Graham share the distinction of winning silverware both as players and managers for their clubs – each winning nine trophies.
But when it comes to winning the trophy that really counts – the First Division title – George Graham was more successful than Spurs' biggest legend.

	George Graham	Bill Nicholson
League titles	1971, 1981, 1989	1951, 1961
FA Cup	1971, 1993	1961, 1962, 1967
League Cup	1987, 1993	1971, 1973
Europe	1970, 1994	1963, 1972

They Managed Both Clubs

GEORGE GRAHAM

George Graham was a successful manager
for Spurs, guiding them to their first trophy
in eight years and UEFA Cup qualification.
He was better for Arsenal.

	Arsenal	Spurs
Matches	460	126
League titles	2	0
FA Cup	1	0
League Cup	2	1
Cup-Winners Cup	1	0

Oh, Rocky, Rocky!

Wednesday 4 March 1987, White Hart Lane,
League Cup semi-final replay

Spurs 1
Allen

v

Arsenal 2
Allinson , Rocastle

In 1987 Spurs should have been better than
Arsenal. They had Ossie Ardiles, Glenn Hoddle,
Chris Waddle and Clive Allen, who puts Spurs in
front for the third time in this tie.

Arsenal's team is a mixture of experienced
quality, emerging youth and journeymen like Ian
Allinson, who comes on as a sub and equalizes
with eight minutes to go.

Jewel in the crown of Arsenal's youth is David
Rocastle, and inside the last minute he pokes the
ball home to put Arsenal ahead for the first time
in the whole of the three matches and win the
game. Cue pandemonium on the terraces.

You Can Buy What After the Game?

Sunday 1 March 1987, White Hart Lane,
League Cup semi-final 2nd leg

Spurs 1
Allen

v

Arsenal 2
Anderson , Quinn

Spurs had won the first game at Highbury 1-0
thanks to a Clive Allen goal, and in this 2nd leg,
Allen again puts them 1-0 up (2-0 on aggregate).
An announcement comes over the tannoy at
half-time telling Spurs fans how they can buy
their tickets for the final.
Has a premature ejaculation ever turned out to
be quite as embarrassing as that one?
Viv Anderson and Niall Quinn score the goals to
take the match to a deciding replay.

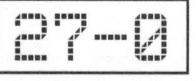

DAVID BENTLEY

David Bentley could barely make the subs bench for the Gunners, though he still managed a better goals-per-game ratio for Arsenal than he did at Spurs.

But it's off the pitch where the Bentley story gets interesting.

After picking up an undisclosed fee from Blackburn Rovers for Bentley, Arsenal would score financially again. Relative success at Rovers suckered Spurs into paying a ludicrous £15m for the player, of which Arsenal trousered a whopping £7m. Spurs would eventually let the disappointing Bentley go for nothing.

Gunners

Lilywhites

25-0

European Giants

Study the record books and you'll need a magnifying glass to find Spurs' big European away wins. They won at AC Milan and Ajax, but then so have Arsenal, who scored more goals in the process.

Here are a few of Arsenal's recent European adventures, at places where Spurs have never tasted victory:

Inter 1-**5 Arsenal**
2003

Roma 1-**3 Arsenal**
2002

Real Madrid 0-**1 Arsenal**
2006

Juventus 0-**1 Arsenal**
1980

Bayern Munich 0-**2 Arsenal**
2013

24-0

Spursday

MONDAY

TUESDAY

WEDNESDAY

SPURSDAY

FRIDAY

SATURDAY

SUNDAY

Monday, Tuesday, Wednesday . . . Spursday.
The fourth day of the week, once known as Thursday,
is now more commonly known as Spursday in
north London because that's when Spurs play their
European games. Arsenal stick to Tuesdays and
Wednesdays when the Champions League is on.

23–0

'Look at That, Ooooh, Look at That!'

Saturday 23 December 1978, White Hart Lane, Division One

Spurs 0

v

Arsenal 5

Sunderland (3), Stapleton , Brady

It's Christmas 1978 and Arsenal fans are hoping for some extra festive cheer as they visit newly promoted Spurs.

Alan Sunderland scores a hat-trick, but the man of the match is Liam Brady, who steals the show with a goal that will be played over and over again on TV for years to come. Robbing Peter Taylor 25 yards out, Brady steadies himself on the edge of the area and strokes the ball with the outside of his magical left foot, curling it past the hapless Mark Kendall.

'Look at that, ooooh look at that! What a goal from Brady!' shrieks John Motson.

Jingle bells, jingle bells . . .

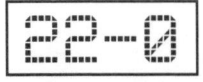

995

```
000000000   000000000   000000000
000000000   000000000   000000000
000    000  000    000  000
000    000  000    000  000
000    000  000    000  000
000000000   000000000   000000000
000000000   000000000   000000000
        000         000         000
        000         000         000
        000         000         000
000000000   000000000   000000000
000000000   000000000   000000000
```

In 2006 Arsenal broke the record for the most
consecutive Champions League games (10)
without conceding a goal. No one breached the
Gunners' defence for 995 minutes.
That's more minutes than Spurs have played in
all their Champions League group and knockout
matches put together.

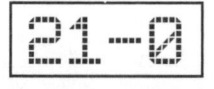

Champions League
Qualification

Since the Champions League started in 1992,
Arsenal have qualified a total of 17 times, with
qualification for the 2014/15 competition also
making it 17 times in a row. Spurs have qualified
just the once.

20–0

Oceans Apart

In the Hollywood blockbuster *Ocean's Twelve*, George Clooney and Brad Pitt successfully escape from authorities in Amsterdam by leaving their hotel wearing Arsenal tracksuits and caps. Being disguised as Spurs players in Europe would have been unconvincing.

Lasagnegate

In 2005 Arsenal had to wait until the last match of the season to celebrate St Totteringham's Day. Spurs were ahead in the table and only had to match Arsenal's result in the final game to qualify for the Champions League for the first time. But on the morning of the game, half the Spurs team shat themselves, blaming it on dodgy lasagne they'd had the night before.

A failed attempt to postpone their game left them having to drag themselves around the Upton Park pitch with buttocks clenched. West Ham took advantage to win 2-1.

A Thierry Henry hat-trick, meanwhile, gave Arsenal a 4-2 win over Wigan, meaning the Gunners leapfrogged Spurs to clinch the final Champions League spot. Gutwrenching.

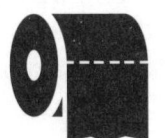

18--0

St Totteringham's Day

This is the name given to the day when Arsenal are guaranteed to finish above Spurs in the table. In recent decades you could say that's the first day of the season, but we're talking mathematical guarantees here.

In 2004, St Totteringham's Day fell on 13 March, a full 10 games before the end of the season. Arsenal have been able to celebrate St Totteringham's Day in every one of the last 19 seasons, and there's no sign of that changing any time soon.

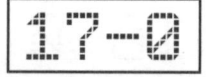

The Original 1-0 to the Arsen:

Spurs **0**

v

Arsenal **1**

Kennedy

It's the last game of the 1970/71 season and Arsenal are chasing the double. A 0-0 draw will be good enough to give the Gunners the title, but two minutes from time 19-year-old Ray Kennedy heads the winner past Pat Jennings and Arsenal have clinched the title at the home of their rivals.

Winning the league at home is glorious, but winning it in front of the enemy is twice as nice.

Snoring, Snoring Tottenham

'I tried to watch the Tottenham match on television in my hotel yesterday, but I fell asleep.'

ARSENE WENGER

15-0

Boring, Boring Arsenal

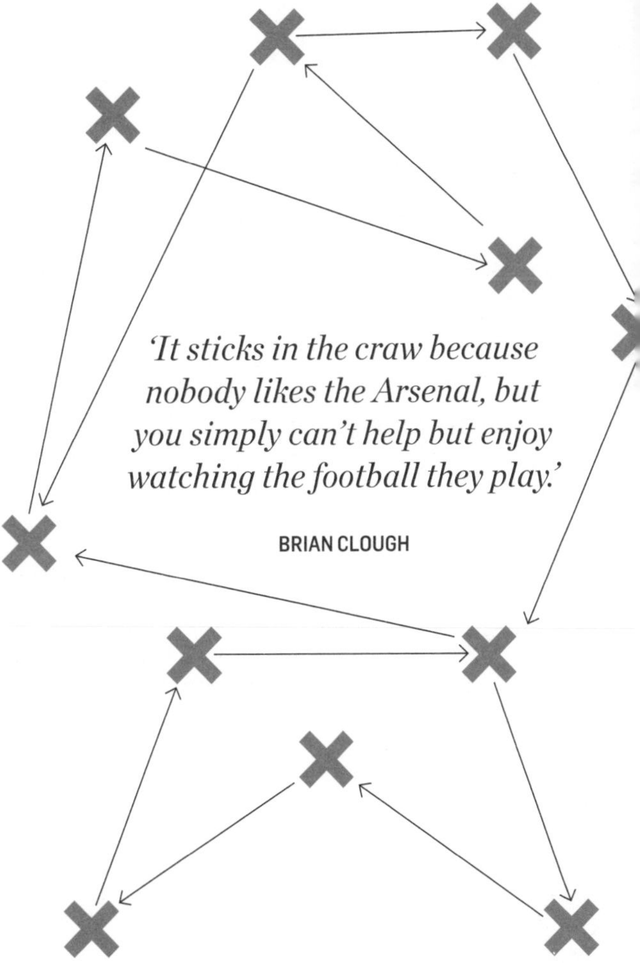

*'It sticks in the craw because
nobody likes the Arsenal, but
you simply can't help but enjoy
watching the football they play.'*

BRIAN CLOUGH

No Show

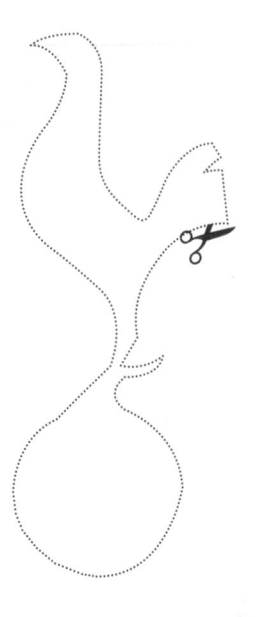

In 1978, Spurs failed to show up for the
annual league fixture at Highbury.
They were in Division Two at the time.

Treble Chasers

Saturday October 20 1934, Highbury, Division One

Arsenal **5**

Scorers unrecorded

v

Spurs **1**

Arsenal have been League champions two seasons running, so they're full of confidence going into this campaign's first north London derby. The home fans are treated to a majestic 5-1 victory, which remains Arsenal's biggest home win over Spurs. Spurs will endure another thrashing in the return fixture (see 72-0) as Arsenal go on to lift the league title again.

The Big Five

ARSENAL
CHELSEA
LIVERPOOL
MAN CITY
MAN UTD

11-0

Home

THE EMIRATES
Capacity: 60,361

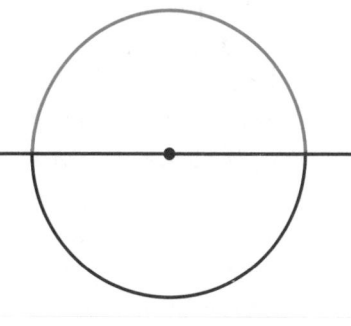

WHITE HART LANE
Capacity: 36,240

Mind you, Spurs are planning a new ground that's going to house 56,250. Close, but no cigar.

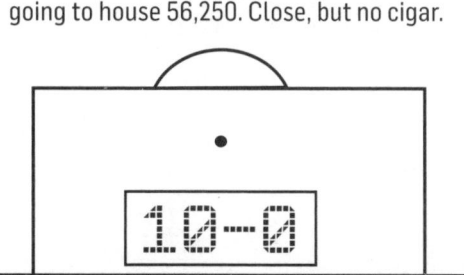

By Royal Appointment

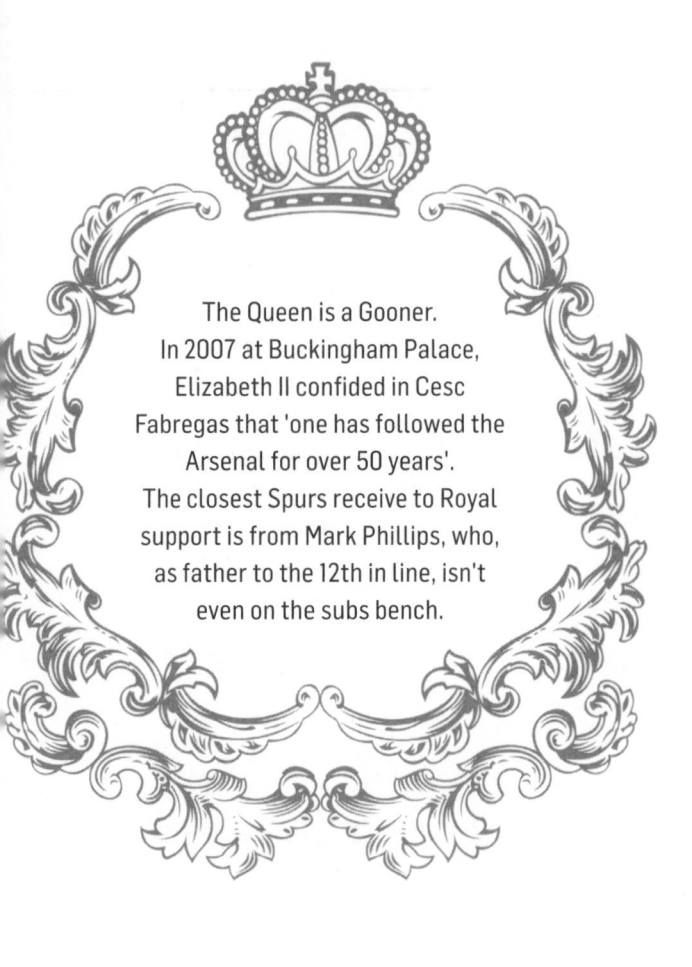

The Queen is a Gooner.
In 2007 at Buckingham Palace,
Elizabeth II confided in Cesc
Fabregas that 'one has followed the
Arsenal for over 50 years'.
The closest Spurs receive to Royal
support is from Mark Phillips, who,
as father to the 12th in line, isn't
even on the subs bench.

9--0

The Arsenal
Tottenham

8–0

First Derby

Saturday 22 August 1914, White Hart Lane,
War Relief Fund friendly

Spurs **1**

v

Arsenal **5**

Scorers unrecorded

Arsenal moved to north London in 1913, so this
is recognized as the first real derby.
Arsenal are in the Second Division and Spurs
in the First, but the Gunners still take the local
bragging rights, introducing themselves to the
new neighbourhood with a heavy victory.

WAGs

Tony Adams
and
Caprice
supermodel

Jermain Defoe
and
Imogen Thomas
Big Brother 7

All-Rounders

DENIS COMPTON	GARY LINEKER
CBE	OBE
League (1948) FA Cup (1950)	FA Cup (1991)
England Test cricketer	Leicestershire schools cricketer

In the battle of the *Boys' Own* heroes, both Compton and Lineker scored goals for their clubs and played for England. Both also endorsed consumer products, worked for the BBC and received Palace gongs. But that's where comparisons end. Compton won more silverware in north London and found time to play international cricket, scoring 17 centuries for England.
In Compton's last Test against Australia he made 94, despite having just had his right kneecap removed. Lineker retired from football with a toe injury.

The FA Cup

Let's face it, Spurs are a cup team. The sort of team that can occasionally pull together a run of form for a few games but just aren't good enough to do it for a whole season. So the FA Cup is their thing – they've won it 8 times.
Arsenal have won 11.

League Titles

The true measure of a team's quality is performing
week in, week out, and winning league titles.
No surprise then that Arsenal have won 13
and Spurs 2 (two).
That's the same amount as Burnley and Portsmouth.

First Match

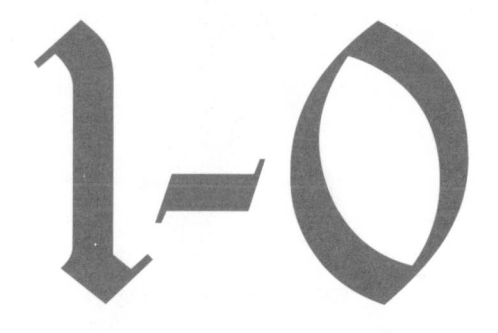

The very first league match between Arsenal and
Spurs was in Football League Division One on
4 December 1909. Not a north London derby this
one – those would start with Arsenal's move to
Highbury – but the scoreline was familiar.
1-0 to The Arsenal.

A is for Arsenal

Even before a ball is kicked at the start of the season, Arsenal sit top of the table on alphabetic order, while Spurs are down around the relegation zone. Come the end of the season, you can be certain that Arsenal will still be looking down on them, as they have every year since 1995.

1–0

ARSENAL
100

SPURS
0

Created and compiled by
Will Brooks and Tim Glynne-Jones

with Alex Perry

BANTAM PRESS

LONDON · TORONTO · SYDNEY · AUCKLAND · JOHANNESBURG

TRANSWORLD PUBLISHERS
61–63 Uxbridge Road, London W5 5SA
A Random House Group Company
www.transworldbooks.co.uk

First published in Great Britain
in 2014 by Bantam Press
an imprint of Transworld Publishers

Created and compiled by Will Brooks and Tim Glynne-Jones with Alex Perry
(Arsenal) copyright © Will Brooks and Tim Glynne-Jones 2014

Design by David Ashford

Visit www.100nil.com for more indefensible screamers.

Will Brooks and Tim Glynne-Jones have asserted their right under the
Copyright, Designs and Patents Act 1988 to be identified as the authors of
this work.

A CIP catalogue record for this book
is available from the British Library.

ISBN 9780593074572

Addresses for Random House Group Ltd companies outside the UK can be found
at: www.randomhouse.co.uk
The Random House Group Ltd Reg. No. 954009

The Random House Group Limited supports the Forest Stewardship Council®
(FSC®), the leading international forest-certification organisation. Our
books carrying the FSC label are printed on FSC®-certified paper. FSC is the
only forest-certification scheme supported by the leading environmental
organisations, including Greenpeace. Our paper procurement policy can be
found at www.randomhouse.co.uk/environment

MIX
Paper from
responsible sources
FSC
www.fsc.org   FSC® C014496

Typeset in Flama

Printed and bound in Germany

2 4 6 8 10 9 7 5 3 1